Mitchell Lane

PUBLISHERS

mitchelllanepub.com

2001 SW 31st Avenue
Hallandale, FL 33009

Copyright © 2026 by Mitchell Lane Publishers. All rights reserved. No part of this book may be reproduced without written permission from the publisher. Printed and bound in the United States of America.

First Edition, 2026.
Author: Tamra B. Orr
Designer: Ed Morgan
Editor: Tammy Gagne

Series: Art and Design Careers
Title: A Career in Photography

Library bound ISBN: 979-8-89260-505-2
eBook ISBN: 979-8-89260-506-9

Photo credits: cover, 11, 25, 27, 31, 33, 35, 39, 43 Shutterstock; contents, p. 5, 7, 9, 13, 17, 19, 21, 23, 29, 37, 41 freepik.com; p. 15 wikimedia

Contents

1	**Capturing a Moment**	4
2	**Drawing With Light**	12
3	**Standing Behind the Lens**	20
4	**Working the Job**	28
5	**Starting Right Now**	34

Glossary	44
Ready, Set, Shoot!	46
Find Out More	47
Index	48
About the Author	48

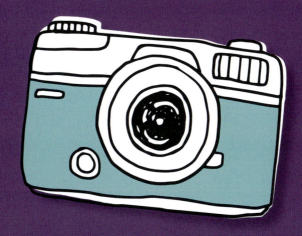

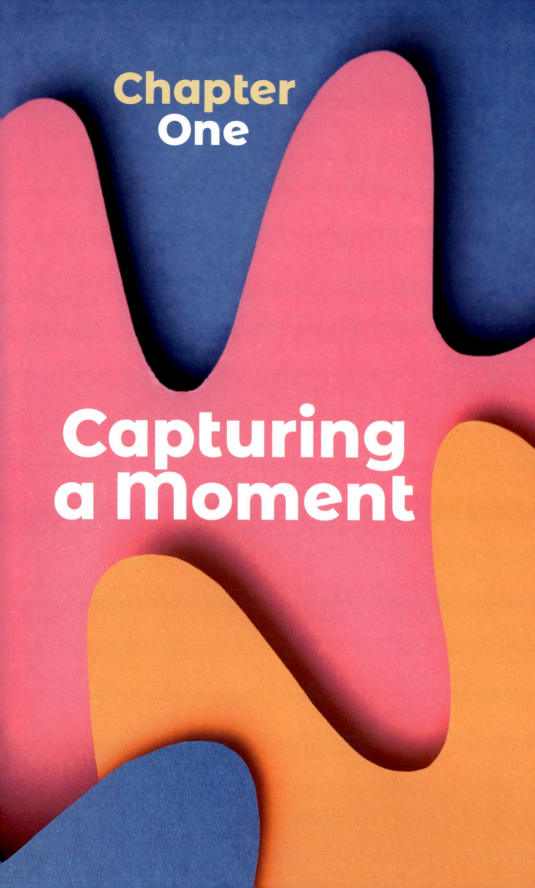

Chapter One

Capturing a Moment

"Run, Josh, run!" shouted Jordan, cheering for his older brother from his seat in the stands. As Josh crossed into the end zone to score a touchdown, Jordan and his parents jumped up and down. The Watsons never missed a football game, and Jordan always enjoyed watching his brother on the field.

"I think the team is going all the way to the state championship this year," said Mr. Watson. Jordan was about to tell his father that he said that every year. But before Jordan could reply, his eye was caught by a woman crouching on the sidelines.

CHAPTER ONE

He wondered what she was doing. After looking more closely, he realized that she held a large camera in her hands. The woman was constantly moving and shifting, squatting down low one moment and stretching up high the next.

"Who is that, Mom?" Jordan asked. Mrs. Watson glanced to where he was pointing. "That's Sharon Henderson," she replied. "She is the local newspaper's sports photographer."

"Remember that great photo of Josh scoring the winning touchdown last year?" Mr. Watson asked. The family had a copy framed for Josh's birthday. "Sharon took that one. Her shots are in almost every edition, in print and online," Mr. Watson added.

Capturing a Moment

Taking pictures of athletes as they run, jump, kick, and score is one of the many wonderful aspects of working as a sports photographer.

CHAPTER ONE

Jordan was intrigued, as he was always taking his own photos with his cell phone. He loved recording moments, whether it was capturing a slice of his favorite pizza or the surprised look on his mother's face when he handed her flowers for her birthday. He had never thought about taking photos for work before. He hadn't even realized it was a career choice.

"Hey Dad, do you think I could meet Ms. Henderson?"

"I don't see why not," Mr. Watson said. Once the band started the halftime show, Jordan and his dad walked over to the photographer. She was still standing near the end zone, fiddling with her camera. She smiled as Jordan walked up.

"Hello, Sharon," said Mr. Watson. "This is my son Jordan."

Capturing a Moment

People who enjoy taking pictures may be able to turn this fun hobby into a lifelong career.

CHAPTER ONE

"Great to meet you, Jordan. That was a thrilling touchdown your brother just made. I was so glad I snapped the picture just as his foot landed in the end zone. I bet this image will make the sports page of the weekend edition."

"What is it like to be a sports photographer?" Jordan asked.

"Oh, I think it is the world's best job. I get to be right in the middle of the sports action," she explained, "and capture the moment, whether it includes scoring a touchdown or crossing a finish line. I think of taking pictures as a way to freeze time," she added.

Jordan grinned. Capturing moments and stopping time. Photography sounded like an amazing career.

Capturing a Moment

Becoming a Sports Photographer

Sports photographers don't have to be athletes, but they'll likely have to run, bend, and jump like one to get the best pictures. Sports photos are typically published both in print and on news and sports websites. Sports photographers often need special lenses to make sure their cameras get clear, up-close pictures of athletes in motion.

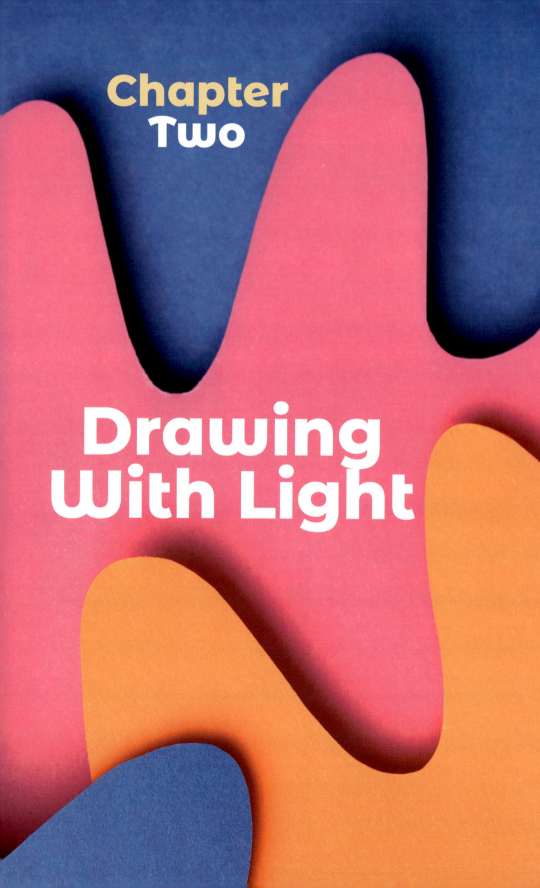

The word *photography* means "drawing with light" in Ancient Greek. This is a fitting description of what taking pictures does. For most of history, the only way to capture an image of a favorite person, place, or thing was to hire an artist. Some artists used pencils while others picked up paintbrushes or a **chisel**. No matter which method the artist used, the process was usually slow and expensive. If the artist was not as talented as hoped, the result might also be disappointing. Today, the average person reaches for a cell phone to take a picture six times a day. In fact, more photos have been taken in the last couple of years than in the entire history of photography.

CHAPTER TWO

In the Beginning

The first cameras were invented in the early to mid-1800s. Their pictures took hours to develop and required special paper and multiple chemicals. By 1889, George Eastman, future founder of Kodak, created the first roll of film. It allowed a photographer to shoot multiple pictures in a row for the first time. Eastman knew the importance of light for good pictures. According to the National Press Photographers Association, he once said, "Light makes photography. Embrace light. Admire it. Love it. But above all, know light. Know it for all you are worth, and you will know the key to photography."

As more inventors became fascinated by cameras, the field of photography grew. In 1936, color photos became possible. A decade later, the first instant camera was produced. From there, cameras got faster and easier to use. By 1974, the first fully-automatic camera was made. Soon, even **disposable** cameras were available.

Drawing With Light

This Susse Frères daguerreotype camera is more than one hundred years old. The only one left today is on display at a camera museum in an Austrian auction house.

CHAPTER TWO

Modern Cameras

By the end of the twentieth century, cameras evolved to the digital format seen today. Thanks to the Internet and social media sites, people can easily share their pictures with a few taps or clicks. Almost 4 billion smartphone users take pictures daily. Experts predict that by 2030, people will take 2.3 trillion photos a year.

People who take the best pictures might be able to make a living as photographers. There are many different **specialties** they can pursue. Professional photographs are needed in a wide range of publications, on the Internet, and for special events such as weddings.

Drawing With Light

Unlike in the past, most people today have a great camera riding around in their pockets or bags. Virtually all cell phones come equipped with cameras.

CHAPTER TWO

Meet the Masters

Over the last century, many photographers have been recognized as masters of the field. These artists found ways to capture a moment in time unlike any other. Ansel Adams was known for taking breathtaking black-and-white landscape photos. Dorothea Lange took pictures of many people who were struggling to survive during the Great Depression (1929–1939). Photographers Annie Leibovitz and Richard Avedon became famous for their **portraits** of models and other celebrities.

Avedon once stated, "I believe that you've got to love your work so much that it is all you want to do." Good advice from a true master. Becoming a professional photographer is not an easy road, but the hard work is worth the chance to stop time for just a moment.

Drawing With Light

Becoming a Nature Photographer

People who love being outdoors and soaking up the beauty of nature often enjoy working as nature photographers. These photographers take pictures of **flora** and **fauna**. Nature photographers are people who see the artistry in sunlight dancing on the trees, the curious face of a squirrel, or the brilliant color of a flower's petals. These images may be used in online magazine articles, calendars, or even advertisements.

Chapter Three

Standing Behind the Lens

There is both good news and bad news for young people interested in a career in photography. The good news is that photographers do not need a formal education. No college degree or certification is required to make a living in this field. The bad news is that photography has a slow career track. Because it can take time to build the experience a photographer needs to get regular jobs, the best time to get started is now.

CHAPTER THREE

Begin by looking into local universities, community colleges, and **vocational** schools. Community centers may offer classes or workshops in photography as well. There are also many online courses available. Topics might range from choosing the right camera to using photography software to learning how to advertise photography services.

More Than a Good Eye

People often say that a photographer needs a good eye. This means being able to recognize the best subjects and ways to photograph them. It is true that the most skilled photographers can take in a view and quickly identify ideal ways to get a perfect shot. According to Canon, Ansel Adams once stated, "A good photograph is knowing where to stand." A good eye, however, still needs to be trained. Photographers must learn the proper techniques to turn photography into a career.

Standing Behind the Lens

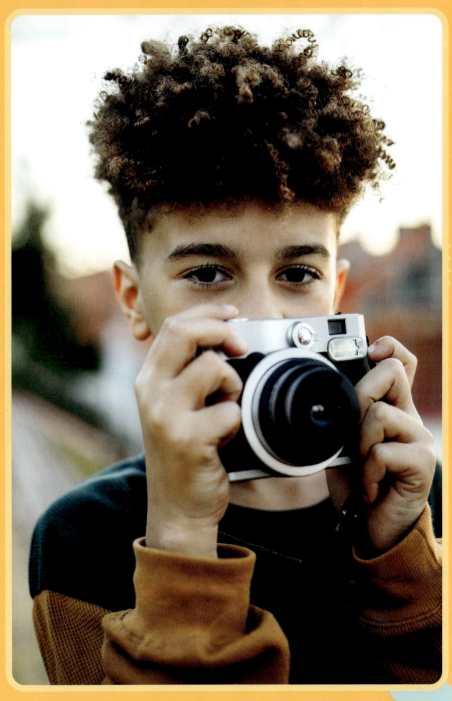

Good photography requires a unique blend of talent, skill, practice, and education. Classes can help turn decent photographers into professional ones.

CHAPTER THREE

Additional skills that photographers need to learn include knowing how to edit photos with a computer, working well with clients, keeping photos organized, and understanding the basics of running a business. These skills can be learned by reading books, talking with other photographers, and taking classes. Many photographers, **amateurs** to professionals, join a professional photography organization such as the Photographic Society of America. This group has been providing webinars, study groups, and other resources for photographers for almost a century.

Learning the Lingo

As with other fields, the photography business has its own vocabulary. Knowing and understanding the most common terms helps photographers get the most out of their cameras. Being familiar with these terms also helps photographers communicate effectively with clients.

Standing Behind the Lens

Computer skills are an essential part of photography. They help people take their photos from good to great.

CHAPTER THREE

While there are dozens of photography terms, some of the most important ones are *aperture*, *focus*, and *shutter speed*. The aperture is the opening that controls the amount of light entering the camera. This affects how much of the photo will be in focus, meaning sharp and clear. The shutter is like a door on a camera's lens. Shutter speed controls the amount of time the shutter remains open to take a photo. This allows a photographer to freeze or blur motion.

It can take time to learn everything a camera can do, and how it all works. Writer and photographer Marianne Stenger wrote an article titled "20 Essential Photography Tips for Beginners" for the *Bob Books* website. In it she shared, "The best way to keep improving is to practice often, make mistakes and be open to learning from others, whether they're well-established photographers or newcomers to the craft."

Standing Behind the Lens

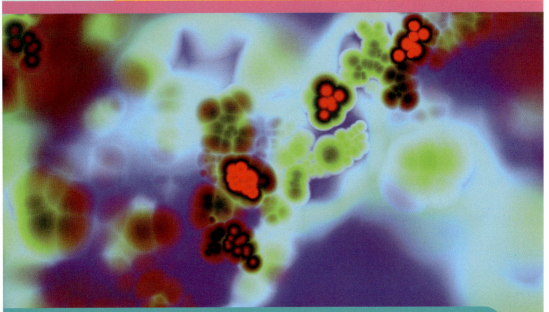

Becoming a Nanoscience Photographer

Some photographers struggle with fitting large images into a small frame. Nanoscience photographers tackle the opposite challenge. Using special, tiny cameras, some attached to microscopes, these people take pictures of items too small to be seen by the naked eye. These images are most often used for medical and scientific purposes, including biology and physics textbooks.

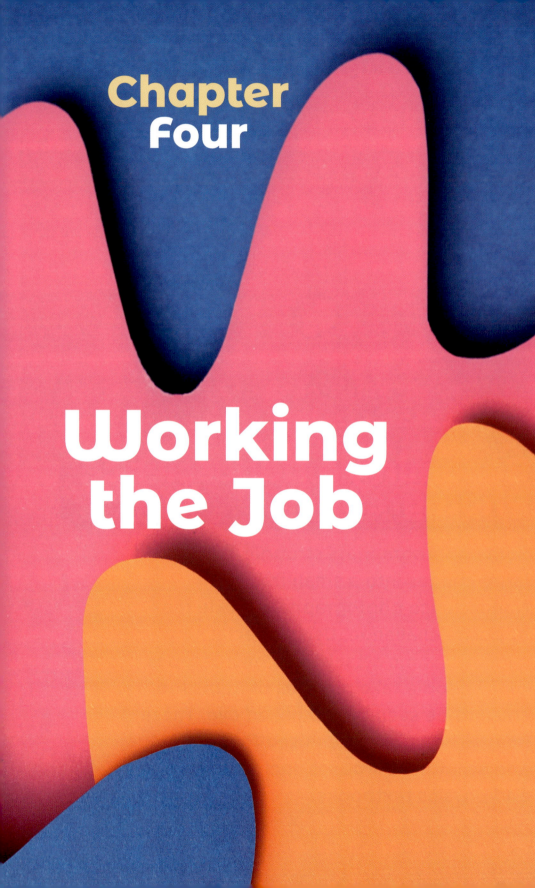

Chapter four

Working the Job

Being a photographer involves taking many pictures, but this is only one step in turning photography from a hobby into a career. Professional photographers are experts. They must learn about each task involved in this complex work to meet their clients' expectations.

Behind the Scenes

Photographers must get familiar with different types of gear. They must know how to add and remove camera lenses and **filters**. Many new photographers cannot afford multiple cameras, so lenses may even need to be swapped in the middle of a shoot. Photographers must also be able to set up lighting equipment, backdrops, and tripods. A tripod is a three-legged mount to keep a camera steady. Photographers should also know how to change all batteries, memory cards, and cords as needed.

CHAPTER FOUR

Photographers must also learn to use photo editing software. These programs help photographers view their images to decide what changes may be necessary. They may want to intensify certain colors or the amount of light. They may want to crop an image or remove objects that clients won't want in a photo. These are just a few of the ways that software helps create better pictures.

The paper and ink used to print photos can also make a big difference in how the finished product looks. A glossy or **matte** finish may suit a particular image better. The best photographers know how to use these tools to make their work look spectacular.

Becoming a Scrapper

While some photographers work for a company, about 64 percent are self-employed. People who work for themselves must learn how to promote themselves. Some experts believe the key to landing that first photography job is finding a specialty.

Working the Job

Knowing how to edit any photograph, including adjusting the lighting and coloring, will help produce the very best pictures.

CHAPTER FOUR

Photographer Rob Baggs wrote on the *Fstoppers* website, "[W]ork out what it is you're good at and what it is you're passionate about." He knows that getting started is a challenge and admits that he refused to give up until someone hired him. "I asked everyone I could find if they knew anyone, and I called in every favor I'd ever **accrued**. You usually need to be a scrapper to get in that first door." Scrappers are people who work hard for what they want.

Self-promotion is incredibly important for any beginning photographer. It is helpful for photographers to have confidence in themselves and their work. Baggs advises, "The world can feel small when you're looking for work, particularly with no experience, but it isn't. Eventually, someone will take a chance on you, and you need to over-deliver like never before."

Working the Job

Becoming a Medical Photographer

Specializing in medical photography takes a steady hand—and a strong stomach. Medical photographers take pictures of injuries, diseases, and surgical procedures. These images are used for education and research and often appear in textbooks or scientific journals.

Chapter
Five

Starting
Right Now

Since photographers do not need a specific degree or certification, young people who are interested in this career can start working toward it at any time. Some people start by donating their services to family members or friends. Others join the staff of a school newspaper. These steps can provide some early experience. Young people can even start looking for simple photography jobs that pay a small amount of cash.

CHAPTER FIVE

Start With a Smartphone

Most new photographers do not need to buy anything in the beginning. Photographer Spencer Cox told the *Photography Life* website, "Use the camera you already have, and don't look back." For most young people, that camera is on a smartphone.

As cell phones have improved, so have their cameras. Some can change focus and adjust lighting. Others may even have multiple lenses. It's easy to use a cell phone to take multiple shots of the same thing, making small adjustments to get the photo just right. Users can see the images immediately, giving them instant feedback. These reasons are likely why 92 percent of today's photos are taken with cell phones.

Starting Right Now

The earliest photographers could never have imagined having a device that takes amazing pictures and fits inside a pocket.

CHAPTER FIVE

Photographers should take pictures daily—and lots of them. It is also important to study the images. Consider what might make each photo better. Photographers who want to invest in a professional camera should do their homework first. James Artaius wrote on the *Digital Camera World* website, "Look for a camera that's not too expensive, is simple to use but capable of advanced shooting to support you while you grow, and above all offers great image quality."

Building a Portfolio

All photographers should have a portfolio. This collection of the artist's best work highlights the photographer's skills and experience. Choose photos that demonstrate good lighting, framing, and staging. The images should also showcase any specialties. Next, decide how to present those photos. Web portfolios upload pictures to a website. A link can be shared with potential clients. Print portfolios are printed photos arranged in a binder and presented at in-person interviews with employers.

Starting Right Now

The Internet has made sharing portfolios easy for many photographers.

CHAPTER FIVE

The Beginning Photography Podcast recommends following the rules of photography without any fear of being unique. "Risks are important in the world of art," an article on the podcast's website states, "and this extends to your portfolio. Don't just put prim and proper shots in there; don't be afraid to take a risk that you think is going to show examples of your creativity and **innovation**, even if it's a little bit outside the box." Some professionals also suggest adding a business card, self-portrait, and brief bio.

Starting Right Now

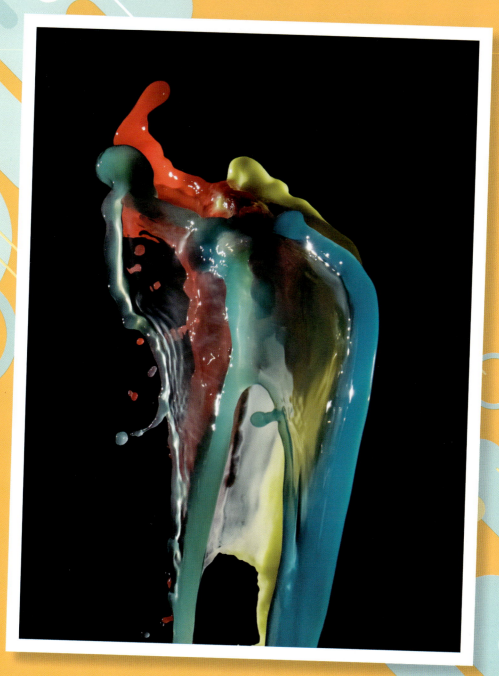

One of the best skills a photographer can develop is seeing the value in images that others might totally overlook.

CHAPTER FIVE

Becoming a photographer requires hard work and dedication. But for people with a passion for this art form, there is nothing like freezing that moment in time. Photography is indeed as much an art form as any other. As a famous quote by photographer Peter Adams states, "Photography is not about cameras, gadgets, and gizmos. Photography is about photographers. A camera didn't make a great picture any more than a typewriter wrote a great novel."

Starting Right Now

Becoming an Extreme Weather Photographer

When other people are running away from danger, weather photographers run toward it. They capture the most intense forms of weather, such as heavy rain from hurricanes and the spinning winds of tornadoes. Photographers who love adventure—and don't mind getting wet and dirty—may be perfect for this career option.

Glossary

accrued
Gathered over time

amateurs
People who take part in an activity for fun and not for payment

chisel
A tool with a sharp edge that is used for carving

disposable
Good for just one or a few uses before the item must be thrown away

fauna
The wild animals in a specific region

filters
Devices placed over a camera lens to change the look of a photo, or effects applied to photos during computer editing

flora
The plants in a specific region

innovation
The use of creativity and knowledge to create something new

matte
Having a flat or glare-free image

portraits
Likenesses of people, often focusing on their faces

specialties
Areas of exceptional skill or training

vocational
Related to a skilled trade

Ready, Set, Shoot!

Test your new knowledge of photography by answering the following questions.

1. A person who takes pictures at football games for a newspaper is called a:

    A. Nanoscience photographer

    B. Sports photographer

    C. Extreme weather photographer

2. When did color photography become possible?

    A. The mid-1800s

    B. 1936

    C. 1974

3. What is the opening that controls how much light can enter a camera called?

    A. Aperture

    B. Lens

    C. Shutter

4. What percentage of photographers are self-employed?

    A. 15 percent

    B. 37 percent

    C. 64 percent

Answers: B, B, A, C

Find Out More

IN PRINT

Coffelt, Nancy. *A Career in Film and Video*. Mitchell Lane Publishers, 2026.

The Beginner's Photography Guide: The Ultimate Step-by-Step Manual for Getting the Most from Your Digital Camera. DK Books, 2024.

Valenzuela, Roberto. *The Successful Professional Photographer: How to Stand Out, Get Hired, and Make Real Money as a Portrait or Wedding Photographer*. Rocky Nook, 2020.

ON THE INTERNET

Photography Life, n.d.
https://photographylife.com/photography-tips-for-beginners

Professional Photographers of America, n.d.
www.ppa.com

Photographic Society of America, n.d.
https://psa-photo.org

Index

Adams, Ansel, 18, 22
aperture, 26
Avedon, Richard, 18
cell phone cameras, 8, 13, 16, 36
color photography, 14
digital cameras, 16
disposable cameras, 14
early cameras, 14
education, 21, 22
extreme weather photography, 43
filters, 29
focus, 26, 36
Lange, Dorothea, 18
Leibovitz, Annie, 18
lenses, 11, 29, 36
medical photography, 33
nanoscience photography, 27
nature photography, 19
photo editing software, 24, 30
portfolios, 38, 40
portraits, 18, 40
printing photos, 30
shutter speed, 26
sports photography, 6, 11
taking risks, 40

About the Author

Tamra B. Orr is a full-time writer living in the Pacific Northwest. She is the author of more than 750 books for readers of all ages. She and her family are all known to take numerous pictures with their cell phones, especially since Oregon is such a scenic state. In addition, Orr is best friends with a wonderful photographer who is nice enough to share her best shots.